French Folk Songs

FRENCH FOLK SONGS

by Colette Crosnier

THE LANGUAGE SOURCE

Madison, Connecticut

FRENCH FOLK SONGS

Copyright ©1992 by Jeffrey Norton Publishers
All rights reserved.
Printed in the United States of America.

No part of this publication may be reproduced, stored in a retrieval system, or transmitted, in any form or by any means, electronic, mechanical, photocopying, recording, or otherwise, without the prior permission of the publisher.

ISBN: 0-88432-493-1 (Cassette and Book)
ISBN: 0-88432-499-0 (Book only)

Published by Audio-Forum
a division of Jeffrey Norton Publishers, Inc.
On-the-Green, Guilford, CT 06437

TABLE DES MATIERES (Table of Contents)

INTRODUCTION	7
YOUKAIDI (Youkaidi)	9
A LA VOLETTE (Fly away)	11
GENTIL COQU'LICOT (Sweet poppy)	13
VOICI LA SAINT-JEAN (The feast of St. John)	15
EN PASSANT PAR LA LORRAINE (While passing through Lorraine)	17
LA BOURREE EN AUVERGNE (The bourrée in Auvergne)	19
TROIS JEUNES TAMBOURS (Three young drummers)	21
LE COUCOU (The cuckoo)	23
LE PASTOURIAU (The shepherd)	25
IL PLEUT, IL PLEUT BERGERE (It's raining, it's raining shepherdess)	27
COMPERE GUILLERI (Old Man Guilleri)	29
SUR LA ROUTE DE LOUVIERS (On the road to Louviers)	31
NOEL DES BERGERS (Christmas of the shepherds)	33
MA NORMANDIE (My Normandy)	35
AUPRES DE MA BLONDE (Beside my blond)	37
JEAN DE LA LUNE (John of the moon)	39
LE VIEUX CHALET (The old chalet)	41
CADET ROUSSELLE (Cadet Rousselle)	43
LA MARCHE DES ROIS (The march of the kings)	45
LES COMPAGNONS DE LA MARJOLAINE (The companions of the Marjolaine)	47
A LA CLAIRE FONTAINE (At the clear fountain)	49
SAVEZ-VOUS PLANTER LES CHOUX? (Do you know how to plant cabbages?)	51
LES NOCES DU PAPILLON (The wedding of the butterfly)	53
MON PERE M'A DONNE UN MARI (My father gave me a husband)	55
BRAVE MARIN (Brave sailor)	57
LUNDI MATIN (Monday morning)	59
LE ROI ET LA MARQUISE (The king and the marquise)	61
LE CHANT DES ADIEUX (The farewell song - Auld Lang Syne)	63
NOTES	64

Introduction

Songs have always been a traditional part of French culture. For centuries it has been said that "En France, tout finit par des chansons" (In France, everything ends in songs): Folk songs from the various provinces, rounds, canons, marching songs, sea chanties, satirical tunes, love ballads that recount happy or sad stories. The characters are kings, princesses, peasants, soldiers, shepherds, villagers...through them, French history comes alive.

Undoubtedly, the ability to listen well is one of the most important factors in learning a foreign language. While it is fairly simple, in speaking, to trip over such words as "cœur," "étais," and "porte" with doubtful diction, the moment the duration of a word is prolonged, as in singing, the ear can readily detect the faulty sounds. With a little care, clean pure vowel sounds can be produced.

When speaking French, Anglophones often fail to articulate using the lips and to open the mouth. However, since both of these actions are necessary to tone production, the difficulty is partially overcome by the act of singing. The Anglophone is thus greatly aided by singing in French, for the intonation and stress of the French language, often undiscerned in normal speech, is more evident in singing. The singer unconsciously retains the rhythm, made natural by note values, and accent improves.

Youkaidi

A very popular song with summer camp counselors, who have adapted the words to this old student song.

At the first rays of the sun
Youkaidi, youkaida
The campers come briskly out of their tents,
Singing:

(refrain)
Youkaidi, kaidi, kaida
Youkaidi, youkaida
Youkaidi, kaidi, kaida
Youkaidi, kaida

Then it's assembly time
Youkaidi, youkaida
Knapsacks in place, let's go
We take off with courage
Carrying our gear

Honor is our pride
Youkaidi, youkaida
A kind heart our wealth
Straight ahead, proudly, fearlessly
The camper marches along

We are always happy
Youkaidi, youkaida
Rain or shine
"Sound health, good humor"
Is the camper's motto

The moral of all this
Youkaidi, youkaida
Ladies and gentleman
Is that on this earth
It's better to have fun than to be idle

Youkaïdi

Aux premiers feux du soleil
Youkaïdi, youkaïda
Tout le camp est en éveil
Youkaïdi, kaïda
On voit sortir de la tente
La troupe alerte qui chante:

(refrain)
Youkaïdi, kaïdi, kaïda
Youkaïdi, youkaïda
Youkaïdi, kaïdi, kaïda
Youkaïdi, kaïda

Puis, c'est le rassemblement,
Youkaïdi, youkaïda
Sac au dos et en avant
Youkaïdi, kaïda
Nous partons avec courage
Transportant notre bagage

L'honneur est notre noblesse
Youkaïdi, youkaïda
Un bon cœur notre richesse
Youkaïdi, kaïda
Tout droit, fièrement sans peur
Ainsi marche le campeur

Nous sommes toujours contents
Youkaïdi, youkaïda
Qu'il pleuve ou fasse beau temps
Youkaïdi, kaïda
"Bon pied, bon oeil, bonne humeur"
Est la devise du campeur

La morale de tout ceci
Youkaïdi, youkaïda
Mesdames, messieurs, la voici: Youkaïdi, kaïda
C'est qu'il vaut mieux sur la terre s'amuser que ne rien faire

Fly away

A sweet ditty as light as the bird it describes.

My little bird flew off
Landed on an orange tree

The branch was dry
The branch broke

My little bird
Did you hurt yourself?

I broke my wing
And twisted my foot

My little bird
Will you take care of yourself?

I want to take care of myself and to get married
Get married quickly on an orange tree

A la volette

Mon petit oiseau a pris sa volée (bis)
A pris sa, à la volette (bis)
A pris sa volée

Est allé se mettre sur un oranger (bis)
Sur un o, à la volette (bis)
Sur un oranger

La branche était sèche, la branche a cassé (bis)
La branche a, à la volette (bis)
La branche a cassé

Mon petit oiseau, où t'es-tu blessé? (bis)
Où t'es-tu, à la volette (bis)
Où t'es-tu blessé?

J'me suis cassé l'aile et tordu le pied (bis)
Et tordu, à la volette (bis)
Et tordu le pied

Mon petit oiseau, veux-tu te soigner? (bis)
Veux-tu te, à la volette (bis)
Veux-tu te soigner?

Je veux me soigner et me marier (bis)
Et me ma, à la volette (bis)
Et me marier

Me marier bien vite sur un oranger (bis)
Sur un o, à la volette (bis)
Sur un oranger

Sweet poppy

This charming, lively tune comes to us from the province of Touraine, "Le Jardin de la France." It dates from the reign of Louis XV (1715-1774), who loved to spend his leisure time in the elegant castles of the Loire region. It must be there that he received the gentle advice of the nightingale.

I went down to my garden
To pick some rosemary

Pretty poppy, ladies
Pretty, fresh poppy

To pick some rosemary
I had just picked three sprigs

When a nightingale flew down upon my hand
He told me three verses in Latin

That men aren't worth anything
And boys are worth even less

About the ladies, he didn't say anything
But he praised the maidens highly

Gentil coqu'licot

J'ai descendu* dans mon jardin (bis)
Pour y cueillir du romarin

(refrain)
Gentil coqu'licot, mesdames
Gentil coqu'licot nouveau!

Pour y cueillir du romarin (bis)
J' n'en avais pas cueilli trois brins

Qu'un rossignol vint sur ma main (bis)
Il me dit trois mots en latin

Que les hommes ne valent rien (bis)
Et les garçons encore bien moins!

Des dames, il ne me dit rien (bis)
Mais des d'moiselles beaucoup de bien

*<u>Note</u>: In modern French, it is correct to say, "Je suis descendu dans mon jardin." However, the original text uses "J'ai descendu... ."

The feast of St. John

The feast of St. John, celebrated at mid-June, heralds the summer season. An old traditional folk song from the Vendée region.

1
Here's the feast of St. John
It's a beautiful day
All our friends will gather

(refrain)
Go friend, go
The moon is rising,
Go friend, go
The moon is going away

2
All our friends will gather
Mine won't be here
And I am so sad

3
Mine won't be here
And I am so sad
He is in the battlefields
Over there, in the army

4
He is in the battlefields
Over there, in the army
His face in the wind
His hair ruffled up

5
His face in the wind
His hair ruffled up
--Mine is in Paris
Shopping around

6
Mine is in Paris
Shopping around
--What will he bring back
Pretty one?

7
What will he bring back
Pretty one?
--He will bring me back
A golden belt

8
He will bring me back
A golden belt
A silver ring
And his love forever more

Voici la Saint-Jean

1
Voici la Saint-Jean
la belle journée (bis)
Nos amis seront
Tous à l'assemblée

(refrain)
Va, mon ami va
La lune se lève
Va, mon ami va
La lune s'en va

2
Nos amis seront
Tous a l'assemblée (bis)
Le mien n'y est pas
J'en suis désolée

3
Le mien n'y est pas
J'en suis désolée
Il est dans les champs
Là-bas à l'armée

4
Il est dans les champs
Là-bas à l'armée
La figure au vent
Chev'lure dépeignée

5
La figure au vent
Chev'lure dépeignée (bis)
--L'mien est à Paris
Chercher ma livrée

6
L'mien est à Paris
Chercher ma livrée (bis)
--Que t'apportera-t-il
Mignonne tant aimée?

7
Que t'apportera-t-il
Mignonne tant aimée?
--Il doit m'apporter
Une ceinture dorée

8
Il doit m'apporter
Une ceinture dorée (bis)
Un anneau d'argent
Et sa foi jurée

Passing through Lorraine

A marching song from the province of Lorraine. A shepherdess dreams of becoming a queen: a queen in wooden shoes!

While passing through Lorraine
With my wooden shoes
I met three captains
With my wooden shoes

They called me a peasant
With my wooden shoes

I am not a peasant
With my wooden shoes
Because the King's son loves me
With my wooden shoes

For a New Year's present he gave me
With my wooden shoes
A pretty verbena plant
With my wooden shoes

I planted it down on the plain
With my wooden shoes
If it blooms I'll be a queen
With my wooden shoes

And if it dies
I'll have wasted my time
With my wooden shoes

En passant par la Lorraine

1
En passant par la Lorraine
Avec mes sabots (bis)
Rencontrai trois capitaines
Avec mes sabots dondaine
Oh, oh, oh! avec mes sabots!

2
Rencontrai trois capitaines
Avec mes sabots (bis)
Ils m'ont appelée vilaine
Avec mes sabots dondaine
Oh, oh, oh! avec mes sabots!

3
Ils m'ont appelée vilaine
Avec mes sabots (bis)
Je ne suis pas si vilaine
Avec mes sabots dondaine
Oh, oh, oh! avec mes sabots!

4
Je ne suis pas si vilaine
Avec mes sabots (bis)
Puisque le fils du roi m'aime
Avec mes sabots dondaine
Oh, oh, oh! avec mes sabots!

5
Puisque le fils du roi m'aime
Avec mes sabots (bis)
Il m'a donné pour étrennes
Avec mes sabots dondaine
Oh, oh, oh! avec mes sabots!

6
Il m'a donné pour étrennes
Avec mes sabots (bis)
Un joli pied de verveine
Avec mes sabots dondaine
Oh, oh, oh! avec mes sabots!

7
Un joli pied de verveine
Avec mes sabots (bis)
Je l'ai planté dans la plaine
Avec mes sabots dondaine
Oh, oh, oh! avec mes sabots!

8
Je l'ai plongé dans la plaine
Avec mes sabots (bis)
S'il fleurit je serai reine
Avec mes sabots dondaine
Oh, oh, oh! avec mes sabots!

9
S'il fleurit je serai reine
Avec mes sabots (bis)
Et s'il meurt je perds ma peine
Avec mes sabots dondaine
Oh, oh, oh! avec mes sabots!

The bourrée in Auvergne

The bourrée is a dance from the province of Auvergne.

The bourree in Auvergne
Is doing well
We dance it four by four
Four young and handsome shepherds
We dance it four by four
Around the house

Families dance it together
In the village courtyards
Boys and girls dance it
Their eyes bright with excitement
Boys and girls
Underneath the elm trees

On wedding days
The bourree is everywhere
In the center of the village
Everybody mingles
In the middle of the village
We dance like crazy

La bourrée en Auvergne

La bourrée en Auvergne
La bourrée y va bien (bis)
Nous la dansons à quatre
Quatre jeunes et beaux pâtres
Nous la dansons à quatre
Autour d'une maison

Elle se danse en famille
Dans les cours des hameaux (bis)
Les garçons et les filles
En ont les yeux qui brillent
Les garçons et les filles
Dansant sous les ormeaux

Les jours de mariage
La bourrée est partout (bis)
Au milieu du village
Tout le monde s'engage
Au milieu du village
Nous dansons comme des fous

Three young drummers

A military song from Ile-de-France, popular with the armies of Louis XV around 1760.

Three young drummers were returning from war
Et ri et ran, ran pa ta plan
Were returning from war

The youngest one has a rose in his mouth
Et ri et ran, ran pa ta plan
Has a rose in his mouth

The king's daughter was at her window

Handsome drummer, give me your rose

King's daughter, give me your heart

Handsome drummer, ask my father for it.

Sire, give me your daughter

Handsome drummer, you are not rich enough

I have three ships on the beautiful sea

One full of gold, the other full of precious stones

And the third one for my sweetheart to sail

Handsome drummer, you shall have my daughter

Sire, I thank you, in my country there are prettier ones

Trois jeunes tambours

1
Trois jeunes tambours
S'en revenaient de guerre (bis)
Et ri et ran, ran pa ta plan
S'en revenaient de guerre

2
Le plus jeune a
Dans sa bouche une rose (bis)
Et ri et ran, ran pa ta plan
Dans sa bouche une rose

3
La fille du roi
Etait à sa fenêtre (bis)

4
Joli tambour
Donnez-moi votre rose (bis)

5
Fille du roi
Donnez-moi votre cœur (bis)

6
Joli tambour
D'mandez -le z'a mon père (bis)

7
Sire le roi
Donnez-moi votre fille (bis)

8
Joli tambour
Tu n'es pas assez riche (bis)

9
J'ai trois vaisseaux
Dessus la mer jolie (bis)

10
L'un chargé d'or
L'autre de pierreries (bis)

11
Et le troisième
Pour promener ma mie (bis)

12
Joli tambour
Tu auras donc ma fille (bis)

13
Sire le roi
Je vous en remercie (bis)

14
Dans mon pays
Y en a de plus jolies (bis)

The cuckoo

This amusing song dates back to the 16th century. Its humor is based on the whimsical play of similar sounds in French.

As I was passing by a little wood
Where the cuckoo was singing
In his pretty song he was saying:
Coucou, coucou
And I thought he was saying: Wring his neck!

(refrain)
And I ran,
And I ran away

As I was passing by a pond
Where the ducks were singing
In their pretty song they were saying:
Couéan, couéan
And I thought they were saying: Neck in the pond!

As I was passing by a mill
While the wheel was turning
In its pretty song it said:
Tic-tac, tic-tac
And I thought it was saying: Got to catch him!

As I was passing by a house
Where a woman was singing
In her pretty song she said:
Do-do, do-do
And I thought she said: Break his bones!

As I was passing by a convent
Where the monks were singing
In their pretty song they were saying:
Alleluia, alleluia
And I thought they were saying: Hang the guy!

Le coucou

En passant près d'un p'tit bois
Où le coucou chantait (bis)
Dans son joli chant disait:
Coucou, coucou, coucou, coucou!
Et moi, je croyais qu'il disait:
Tords-lui le cou, tords-lui le cou!

(refrain)
Et moi de m'en cour' cour'
Et moi de m'en courir

En passant près d'un étang
Où les canards chantaient (bis)
Et dans leur joli chant disaient:
Couéan, couéan, couéan, couéan!
Et moi, je croyais qu'ils disaient:
L'cou dans l'étang, l'cou dans l'étang!

En passant près d'un moulin
Pendant qu'la roue tournait (bis)
Dans son joli chant elle disait:
Tic-tac, tic-tac, tic-tac, tic-tac!
Et moi qui croyais qu'elle disait:
Faut que j'l'attrape, faut que j'l'attrape!

En passant devant une maison
Où une bonne femme chantait (bis)
Dans son joli chant elle disait:
Do-do, do-do, do-do, do-do!
Et moi, qui croyais qu'elle disait:
Casse-lui les os, casse-lui les os!

En passant près d'un couvent
Où les moines chantaient (bis)
Dans leur joli chant ils disaient:
Alléluia, alléluia!
Et moi qui croyais qu'ils disaient:
Faut pendre le gars, faut pendre le gars!

The shepherd

A peasant song and dance. Its origin dates back to 1660, in the region of Poitiers.

When I lived with my father
As a shepherd apprentice
He placed me out in the moor
To tend the herds

(refrain)
Herds, herds
I didn't have much of a herd
Herds, herds
I didn't have any herd

I hardly had a herd
I only had three lambs
And the wolf of the plain
Ate the biggest one

He was so ravenous
That he left only the skin
He left only the tail
To decorate my hat

But with the bones of the beast
I made myself a flute
To play at the fair
At the village fair

I played at the village dance
Underneath the big elm tree
So young and old could dance
In their wooden shoes

Le pastouriau

Quand j'étais chez mon père
Apprenti pastouriau *(pastoureau)*
Il m'a mis dans la lande
Pour garder les troupiaux *(troupeaux)*

(refrain)
Troupiaux, troupiaux
Je n'en avais guère
Troupiaux, troupiaux
Je n'en avais biaux *(beau)*

Mais je n'en avais guère
Je n'avais qu' trois agneaux
Et le loup de la plaine
M'a mangé le plus biau

Il était si vorace
N'a laissé que la piau *(peau)*
N'a laissé que la queue
Pour mettre à mon chapiau *(chapeau)*

Mais des os de la bête
Me fis un chalumiau *(chalumeau)*
Pour jouer à la fête
A la fête du hamiau (hameau)

Pour faire danser l'village
Dessous le grand ormiau *(ormeau)*
Et les jeunes et les vieilles
Les pieds dans les sabiots *(sabots)*

It's raining, it's raining shepherdess

The words and the music of this song were written during the French Revolution in 1794. The author also created the Republican calendar that went into effect for a few years. The calendar began on September 22 and the months were given names suggesting the seasons of the year: *Floreal*, month of the flowers; *Fructidor*, month of the fruits; *Thermidor*, month of the summer heat; etc..

1
It's raining shepherdess
Call in your white sheep
Let's go to my cottage
Shepherdess, quickly, let's go
I hear the rain falling noisily
On the foliage
Here comes the storm
Lightning is striking

2
Do you hear the thunder?
It's getting louder
Shepherdess, take shelter
To my right
I can see our little house
And here comes my mother
And my sister Anne, who are going
To open the stable

3
Good evening, mother
My sister Anne, good evening
I am bringing my shepherdess
Home tonight
Go and dry off by our fire, my sweet
Sister, keep her company
Come in, little sheep

4
Mother, take care of
Her pretty herd
Give more straw
To her little lamb
It's done. Let's stay with he
There you are!
She is so lovely
Mother, look at her

5
Let's have some supper
Take this chair
This torch will burn
Right by your side
Taste some of this milk
But you're not eating?
The storm did upset you
It's tired you out

Il pleut, il pleut bergère

1
Il pleut, il pleut bergère
Rentre tes blancs moutons
Allons sous ma chaumière
Bergère, vite, allons
J'entends sur le feuillage
L'eau qui tombe à grand bruit
Voici, voici l'orage
Voilà l'éclair qui luit

2
Entends-tu le tonnerre?
Il roule en approchant
Prends un abri bergère
A ma droite en marchant
Je vois notre cabane
Et tiens, voici venir
Ma mère et ma sœur Anne
Qui vont l'étable ouvrir

3
Bonsoir, bonsoir ma mère
Ma sœur Anne, bonsoir
J'amène ma bergère
Près de vous pour ce soir
Va te sécher, ma mie
Auprès de nos tisons
Sœur, fais-lui compagnie
Entrez, petits moutons

4
Soignons bien ô ma mère
Son tant joli troupeau
Donnez plus de litière
A son petit agneau
C'est fait. Allons près d'elle
Eh bien! Donc, te voilà
Ah mon Dieu, qu'elle est belle
Ma mère, voyez-la

5
Soupons; prends cette chaise
Tu seras près de moi
Ce flambeau de mélèze
Brûlera devant toi
Goûte de ce laitage
Mais tu ne manges pas?
Tu te sens de l'orage
Il a lassé tes pas

Old Man Guilleri

A very old song from Britanny about a real character Guilleri, a scoundrel who died around 1608.

There once was a little man
Named Guilleri
Carabi
He went hunting
For partridges

(refrain)
Carabi
Titi Carabi
Toto Carabo
Old Guilleri
Are you going to give up? ("Are you going to let yourself die?")

He climbed a tree
To watch his dogs run
Carabi
The branch broke
And Guilleri fell

He broke his leg
And dislocated his arm
Carabi
The ladies of the hospital
Rushed toward the commotion

One brought some plaster
Another bandages
They bound his leg
And set his arm

To thank the ladies
Guilleri kissed them
Carabi
It proves that women
Know how to make men well

Compère Guilleri

Il était un p'tit homme
Qui s'appelait Guilleri
Carabi
Il s'en fût à la chasse
A la chasse aux perdrix

(refrain)
Carabi
Titi Carabi
Toto Carabo
Compère Guilleri
Te lairas-tu, te lairas-tu, te lairas-tu *(te laisseras-tu)*
Mouri *(mourir)*?

Il monta sur un arbre
Pour voir ses chiens couri *(courir)*
Carabi
La branche vint à rompre
Et Guilleri tombit

Il se cassa la jambe
Et le bras se démit
Carabi
Les dames de l'hôpital
Sont arrivées au bruit

L'une apporte un emplâtre
L'autre de la charpie
Carabi
On lui banda la jambe
Et le bras lui remit

Pour remercier ces dames
Guilleri les embrassit
Carabi
Ça prouve que par les femmes
L'homme est toujours guéri

On the road to Louviers

A song born in the province of Ile-de-France, around 1820, pointing to the gap that separated the working poor from the nobility.

On the road to Louviers
There once was a working man
Who was smashing piles of rocks
To place underneath wheels

A fine lady came passing by
In a beautiful guilded carriage
And she said to him:
Poor working man
What an awful job you have!

The working man answered:
I must feed my sons
For if I were riding
A carriage like you
I wouldn't be smashing rocks!

This answer is noteworthy
On account of its great simplicity
It proves
That the poor
Are poor in spite of themselves

Sur la route de Louviers

Sur la route de Louviers (bis)
Y avait un cantonnier (bis)
Et qui cassait
Des tas d'cailloux
Et qui cassait des tas d'cailloux
Pour mettr' su' l'passage des roues

Une belle dame vint à passer (bis)
Dans un beau carrosse doré (bis)
Et qui lui dit:
Pauv' cantonnier
Et qui lui dit pauv' cantonnier
Tu fais un fichu métier!

Le cantonnier lui répond: (bis)
Faut que j'nourrisse nos garçons (bis)
Car si j'roulais
Carrosse comme vous
Car si j'roulais carrosse comme vous
Je n'casserais pas de cailloux!

Cette réponse se fait r'marquer (bis)
Par sa grande simplicité (bis)
C'est c'qui prouve
Qu' les malheureux
C'est c'qui prouve que les malheureux
S'ils le sont c'est malgré eux

Christmas of the shepherds

This is an old, traditional Christmas song from the Provence region.

Willie, pick up your tambourine
You, Robin, pick up your flute

(refrain)
To the sound of our instruments
Turelurelu, patapatapan
We will celebrate Christmas gaily

Awake shepherds
Quickly, leave your villages

Bundle up in your coats
Run along the hills

Hum a new tune
Make your flocks dance

Noël des bergers

Guillot, prends ton tambourin
Toi, prends ta flûte, Robin (bis)

(refrain)
Au son de nos instruments
Turelurelu, patapatapan
Au son de nos instruments
Nous dirons Noël gaiement

Réveillez-vous, pastoureaux
Vite, quittez vos hameaux (bis)

Couvrez-vous de vos manteaux
Accourez sur le coteau (bis)

Fredonnez un air nouveau
Faites danser vos troupeaux (bis)

My Normandy

This nostalgic song dates back to the 19th century. It expresses the feeling of homesickness of those who left their province to go to work in Paris.

When hope is reborn
And winter has flown away
Under the beautiful skies of our France
When the sun becomes warmer
When nature turns green again
When the swallows have returned
I love to visit my Normandy
It is the land where I was born

I have seen the fields of Switzerland
And her chalets and her glaciers
I have seen the skies of Italy
And Venice and her gondoliers
In paying tribute to each country
I concluded: there is no place
As beautiful as my Normandy
It is the land where I was born

Ma Normandie

Quand tout renaît à l'espérance
Et que l'hiver fuit loin de nous
Sous le beau ciel de notre France
Quand le soleil revient plus doux
Quand la nature est reverdie
Quand l'hirondelle est de retour
J'aime à revoir ma Normandie
C'est le pays qui m'a donné le jour

J'ai vu les champs de l'Helvétie
Et ses chalets et ses glaciers
J'ai vu le ciel de l'Italie
Et Venise et ses gondoliers
En saluant chaque patrie
Je me disais: aucun séjour
N'est plus beau que ma Normandie
C'est le pays qui m'a donné le jour

Beside my blond

One of the oldest and one of the most popular French marching songs. It dates back to 1635, when Louis XIII and Cardinal Richelieu were engaged in war against Austria.

1
In my father's garden
The lilacs are in bloom
All kinds of birds
Come there to nest

(refrain)
Beside my blond
It's good, it's good, it's good
It's good to laugh

2
All kinds of birds
Come there to nest
The quail, the turtledove
And the pretty partridge

3
The quail, the turtledove
And the pretty partridge
And my pretty dove
Who sings day and night

4
And my pretty dove
Who sings day and night
It sings for the girls
Who don't have a husband

5
It sings for the girls
Who don't have a husband
For me, it doesn't sing
Because I have a nice one

6
For me it doesn't sing
Because I have a nice one
--But tell me, my fair one
Where is your husband?

7
But tell me, my fair one
Where is your husband?
He is in Holland, captured

8
He is in Holland
The Dutch captured him
--What would you give, my fair one
For the return of your husband?

9
What would you give, my fair one
For the return of your husband?
I'd give Touraine,
Paris and St. Denis

10
I'd give Touraine,
Paris and St. Denis
The towers of Notre-Dame
And the steeple of my village

11
The towers of Notre-Dame
And the steeple of my village
And my pretty dove
Who sings day and night

Auprès de ma blonde

1
Dans les jardins d'mon père
Les lilas sont fleuris (bis)
Tous les oiseaux du monde
Vienn't y faire leurs nids

(refrain)
Auprès de ma blonde
Qu'il fait bon, fait bon, fait bon
Auprès de ma blonde
Qu'il fait bon de rire*

2
Tous les oiseaux du monde
Vienn't y faire leurs nids (bis)
La caille, la tourterelle
Et la jolie perdrix

3
La caille, la tourterelle
Et la jolie perdrix (bis)
Et ma jolie colombe
Qui chante jour et nuit

4
Et ma jolie colombe
Qui chante jour et nuit (bis)
Elle chante pour les filles
Qui n'ont point de mari

5
Elle chante pour les filles
Qui n'ont point de mari (bis)
Pour moi ne chante guère
Car j'en ai un joli

6
Pour moi ne chante guère
Car j'en ai un joli (bis)
--Mais dites-moi la belle
Où est votre mari?

7
Mais dites-moi ma belle
Où est votre mari? (bis)
Il est dans la Hollande
Les Hollandais l'ont pris

8
Il est dans la Hollande
Les Hollandais l'ont pris (bis)
--Que donneriez-vous la belle
Pour ravoir votre mari?

9
Que donneriez-vous la belle
Pour ravoir votre mari? (bis)
Je donnerais Touraine
Paris et Saint-Denis

10
Je donnerais Touraine
Paris et Saint-Denis (bis)
Les tours de Notre-Dame
Et l'clocher d'mon pays

11
Les tours de Notre-Dame
Et l'clocher d'mon pays (bis)
Et ma jolie colombe
Qui chante jour et nuit

*<u>Note:</u> There are several adaptations of this song. A popular version of the refrain's last line is "Qu'il fait bon dormir." (sleep)

John of the Moon

A charming children's round which dates back to the 18th century.

On a warm spring night
About one hundred years ago
Under a sprig of parsley, quietly
Was born tiny
John of the Moon

He was as tall as a mushroom
Fragile, delicate, small, cute
Dressed in yellow and green
Could chatter like a parrot
John of the Moon

He could be seen sometimes
Driving along the country roads
In a carriage big as a walnut
Drawn by two mice
John of the Moon

When he ventured through the woods
Far and near and everywhere
Blackbirds and finches chirped on their flutes:
John of the Moon

If by chance a small stream stopped his steps
Too tiny to leap over it, he made a bridge
Out of a blade of grass
John of the Moon

Jean de la Lune

Par une tiède nuit de printemps
Il y a bien de cela cent ans
Que sous un brin de persil, sans bruit
Tout menu naquit
Jean de la Lune (bis)

Il était haut comme un champignon
Frêle, délicat, petit, mignon
Et jaune et vert comme un perroquet
Avait bon caquet
Jean de la Lune (bis)

On le voyait passer quelquefois
Dans un coupé grand comme une noix
Et que le long des sentiers fleuris
Traînaient deux souris
Jean de la Lune (bis)

Quand il se risquait à travers bois
De loin, de près, de tous les endroits
Merles, bouvreuils sur leur mirliton
Répétaient en rond:
Jean de la Lune (bis)

Si par hasard s'offrait un ruisseau
Qui l'arrêtait sur place, aussitôt
Trop petit pour le franchir d'un bond
Faisait d'herbe un pont
Jean de la Lune (bis)

The old chalet

This is an old mountain tune from the Alps region.

Way up on the mountain
Used to be an old chalet
White walls, shingled roof
In front of the door an old birch tree
Way up on the mountain
Used to be an old chalet

Way up on the mountain
The old chalet collapsed
Snow and rocks worked together
To tear it down
Way up on the mountain
The old chalet collapsed

Way up on the mountain
When John came to the chalet
He wept, brokenhearted
Over the remains of his happiness
Way up on the mountain
When John came to the chalet

Way up on the mountain
There is a brand-new chalet
For John courageously rebuilt it
Even more beautiful than before
Way up on the mountain
There is a brand-new chalet

Le vieux chalet

Là-haut sur la montagne
L'était un vieux chalet (bis)
Murs blancs, toit de bardeaux
Devant la porte un vieux bouleau
Là-haut sur la montagne
L'était un vieux chalet

Là-haut sur la montagne
Croula le vieux chalet (bis)
La neige et les rochers
S'étaient unis pour l'arracher
Là-haut sur la montagne
Croula le vieux chalet

Là-haut sur la montagne
Quand Jean vint au chalet (bis)
Pleura de tout son cœur
Sur les débris de son bonheur
Là-haut sur la montagne
Quand Jean vint au chalet

Là-haut sur la montagne
L'est un nouveau chalet (bis)
Car Jean d'un cœur vaillant
L'a rebâti plus beau qu'avant
Là-haut sur la montagne
L'est un nouveau chalet

Cadet Rousselle

Some people believe that Cadet Rousselle was a real man who lived in Cambrai, in the north of France. Others think the words were a parody on another song, "Jean de Nivelle." The music was well-known in 1792, at the time of the French Revolution.

Cadet Rousselle owns three houses
That have neither beams nor rafters
They are the homes of swallows
What will you say about Cadet Rousselle?

Ah! Ah! Ah! yes indeed
Cadet Rousselle is a good fellow

Cadet Rousselle owns three coats
Two yellow ones, the other made of gray paper
That's the one he wears when it's freezing
Or when it's raining or when it's hailing

Cadet Rousselle owns three big dogs
One hunts hares, the other one rabbits
The third one runs away when it's called
Just like Jean Nivelle's dog

Cadet Rousselle owns three beautiful cats
Who never catch rats
The third one has no eyeballs
It doesn't need a candle to go up to the attic

Cadet Rousselle has three sons
One is a thief, the other one a rascal
The third one is somewhat of a cheat
He is like Cadet Rousselle

Cadet Rousselle married his three daughters
In three different neighborhoods
The first two aren't pretty
The third one has no brains

Cadet Rousselle

Cadet Rousselle a trois maisons (bis)
Qui n'ont ni poutres, ni chevrons (bis)
C'est pour loger les hirondelles
Que direz-vous d'Cadet Rousselle?

(refrain)
Ah! Ah! Ah! oui vraiment
Cadet Rousselle est bon enfant

Cadet Rousselle a trois habits (bis)
Deux jaunes, l'autre en papier gris (bis)
Il met celui-là quand il gèle
Ou quand il pleut, ou quand il grêle

Cadet Rousselle a trois gros chiens (bis)
L'un court au lièvre, l'autre au lapin (bis)
L'troisième s'enfuit quand on l'appelle
Comme le chien de Jean Nivelle

Cadet Rousselle a trois beaux chats (bis)
Qui n'attrapent jamais les rats (bis)
Le troisième n'a pas de prunelles
Il monte au grenier sans chandelle

Cadet Rousselle a trois garçons (bis)
L'un est voleur, l'autre fripon (bis)
Le troisième est un peu ficelle
Il ressemble à Cadet Rousselle

Cadet Rousselle a marié (bis)
Ses trois filles dans trois quartiers (bis)
Les deux premières ne sont pas belles
La troisième n'a pas de cervelle

The march of the kings

This Christmas song has its origin in Provence. Bizet, the French composer, has used it as a motif in the Arlésienne suite.

This morning, I watched the procession of
Three great kings traveling on a journey
This morning, I watched the procession of
Three great kings on the main road
They were followed first by some great warriors and by
The keepers of the treasure, weighed down with gold
They were followed first by some great warriors
With shields

Astonished by the clamor, I made way
In order to watch the procession
Astonished by the spectacle, I kept on watching from a distance
The shining star before them
Guided the three wise men
The shining star before them
Stopped short when it reached the child

This morning, I watched the procession of
Three great kings traveling on a journey
This morning, I watched the procession of
Three great kings on the main road

La marche des rois

Ce matin, j'ai rencontré le train
De trois grands rois qui allaient en voyage
Ce matin, j'ai rencontré le train
De trois grands rois dessus le grand chemin
Tout chargés d'or, les suivaient d'abord
De grands guerriers et les gardes du trésor
Tout chargés d'or, les suivaient d'abord
De grands guerriers avec leurs boucliers

Ebahi d'entendre ceci, j'me suis rangé pour voir les équipages
Ebahi d'entendre ceci, de loin en loin les ai toujours suivis
L'astre brillant qui était devant
Servait de guide en menant les trois rois mages
L'astre brillant qui était devant
S'arrêta net quand il fût vers l'enfant

Ce matin, j'ai rencontré le train
De trois grands rois qui allaient en voyage
Ce matin, j'ai rencontré le train
De trois grands rois dessus le grand chemin

The companions of the Marjolaine

The companions of the Marjolaine consisted of a group of sixty men under the command of "le chevalier du guet", a sort of night watchman. Every night they patroled the streets of Paris to insure the safety of the city, and also to watch out for fires, at a time when houses were made out of wood.

1
Who is passing by so late at night?
On the quay?

2
It is the night watchman

3
What does he want?

4
A girl to marry

5
Come back at midnight

6
It is past midnight

7
What will you give me?

8
Sufficient gold and jewels

9
I am not interested

10
My heart I'll give you

Les compagnons de la Marjolaine

1
Qu' est-c'qui passe ici si tard
Compagnons de la Marjolaine
Qu' est-c'qui passe ici si tard
Gai, gai, dessus le quai?

2
C'est le chevalier du guet

3
Que demande le chevalier?

4
Une fille à marier

5
Sur les minuit repassez

6
Voilà les minuit passés

7
Qu'est-ce que vous me donnerez?

8
De l'or, des bijoux assez

9
Je n'suis pas intéressée

10
Mon cœur je vous donnerai

At the clear fountain

This song first originated in the 16th century and landed in Canada with Jacques Cartier, when he settled the territory now known as Québec and Montréal. The song returned to Canada via the French soldiers who came to defend "La Nouvelle France" against the English invader.

As I was walking by
The fountain so clear
The water seemed so appealing
That I felt like taking a bath

(refrain)
I've loved you for a long time
I'll never forget you

Under the leaves of an oak
I dried myself
On the highest branch
The nightingale was singing

Sing, nightingale, sing
Your heart is light
Your heart feels like singing
Mine feels like crying

I lost my lover
Unjustly,
For a bouquet of roses
That I refused her

I wish the rose
Were still on the rosebush
And that my sweetheart
Still loved me

A la claire fontaine

A la claire fontaine
M'en allant promener
J'ai trouvé l'eau si belle
Que je m'y suis baigné

(refrain)
Il y a longtemps que je t'aime
Jamais je ne t'oublierai

Sous les feuilles d'un chêne
Je me suis fait sécher
Sur la plus haute branche
Un rossignol chantait

Chante, rossignol, chante
Toi, qui as le cœur gai
Tu as le cœur à rire
Moi, je l'ai à pleurer

J'ai perdu mon amie
Sans l'avoir mérité
Pour un bouquet de roses
Que je lui refusai

Je voudrais que la rose
Fût encore au rosier
Et que ma douce amie
Fût encore à m'aimer

Do you know how to plant cabbages?

Way back in time before the potato, cabbage was the staple of the French peasant's diet. This popular round honors this humble vegetable.

1
Do you know how to plant cabbages
Fashionably
Do you know how to plant cabbages
As we do?

2
We plant them with our finger

3
We plant them with our hand

4
We plant them with our elbow

5
We plant them with our foot

6
We plant them with our knee

7
We plant them with our nose

8
We plant them with our head

9
Do you know how to plant cabbages?

Savez-vous planter les choux?

1
Savez-vous planter les choux
A la mode, à la mode
Savez-vous planter les choux
A la mode de chez nous?

2
On les plante avec le doigt
A la mode, à la mode
On les plante avec le doigt
A la mode de chez nous

3
On les plante avec la main

4
On les plante avec le coude

5
On les plante avec le pied

6
On les plante avec le genou

7
On les plante avec le nez

8
On les plante avec la tête

9
Savez-vous planter les choux?

The wedding of the butterfly

A popular old song for school children.

1
You must get married
Snow white butterfly
You must get married
Before the old mulberry tree

Dear friends, should I get married
Without being persuaded a bit?

2
I, said the snail,
To lodge your butterfly lady
I, said the snail,
I give you my house

What is given goodheartedly
I accept without fuss

3
I have, said the ant,
Some bits of green pods
I have, said the ant,
A few grains of wheat also

What a beautiful wedding feast!
You are really treating your friend

4
As for me, said the golden bee
My dessert will be wonderfull
I, said the golden bee,
I still have some liquid honey

Thanks a lot, sweet bee,
For sharing your treasure!

5
For you I will shine
Said the glow-worm in the g
For you I will shine
You don't need to be
Persuaded any longer

Dear friends
Everything is just right
I want very much
To get married

Les noces du papillon

1
Il faut te marier
Papillon couleur de neige
Il faut te marier
Par devant le vieux mûrier

Chers amis, me marierai-je
Sans me faire un peu prier?

2
Moi, dit le limaçon,
Pour loger ta papillonne
Moi, dit le limaçon,
Je te cède ma maison

Ce qu'un brave cœur me donne
Je l'accepte sans façon

3
J'ai là, dit la fourmi,
Des fragment de vertes cosses
J'ai là, dit la fourmi
Quelques grains de blé aussi

Ah! le beau repas de noces!
Tu régales ton ami

4
Moi, dit l'abeille d'or,
Mon dessert fera merveille
Moi, dit l'abeille d'or,
J'ai du miel liquide encor'

Grand merci, gentille abeille
Qui partage son trésor

5
Pour toi je vais briller
Dit le ver luisant dans l'herbe
Pour toi je vais briller
Ne te fais donc plus prier

Chers amis, tout est superbe,
Je veux bien me marier

My father gave me a husband

This satirical song tells the story of a girl who married against her will, as often happened to the young women of past centuries. The song originated as far back as the 17th century.

1
My father gave me a husband
My goodness! What a man, what a tiny man!
My father gave me a husband
My goodness! What a small man!

2
His coat was made out of a leaf
My goodness! What a man, what a tiny man!
His coat was made out of a leaf
My goodness! What a small man!

3
I picked up a candle and looked for him

4
The cat mistook him for a mouse

5
Oh cat, oh cat! It's my husband!

6
Girls, when you take a husband

7
Don't take him so small

Mon père m'a donné un mari

Mon père m'a donné un mari
Mon Dieu! Quel homme, quel petit homme!
Mon père m'a donné un mari
Mon Dieu! Quel homme, qu'il est petit

D'une feuille on fit son habit
Mon Dieu! Quel homme, quel petit homme!
D'une feuille on fit son habit
Mon Dieu! Quel homme, qu'il est petit

J'pris une chandelle et le cherchis
Mon Dieu! Quel homme, quel petit homme!
J'pris une chandelle et le cherchis
Mon Dieu! Quel homme, qu'il est petit

Le chat l'a pris pour une souris
Mon Dieu! Quel homme, quel petit homme!
Le chat l'a pris pour une souris
Mon Dieu! Quel homme, qu'il est petit

Oh chat, oh chat, c'est mon mari!
Mon Dieu! Quel homme, quel petit homme!
Oh chat, oh chat, c'est mon mari!
Mon Dieu! Quel homme, qu'il est petit

Filles qui prenez un mari
Mon Dieu! Quel homme, quel petit homme!
Filles qui prenez un mari
Mon Dieu! Quel homme, qu'il est petit

Ne le prenez pas si petit
Mon Dieu! Quel homme, quel petit homme!
Ne le prenez pas si petit
Mon Dieu! Quel homme, qu'il est petit

Brave sailor

After years spent under the flags during the endless Napoleonic wars, a sailor returns home and experiences much disappointment. An old-fashioned kind of soap opera!

1
The gallant sailor returns
From the war, gently
Worn out shoes, shabby clothes
Poor sailor, where have you been?

2
Madam, I am returning
From the war, gently
Bring on some white wine
The sailor must have a drink
As he passes through

3
The gallant sailor starts to drink
To drink and to sing
And the beautiful hostess
Starts to cry

4
What's wrong, beautiful hostess?
Do you regret the white wine
That the sailor is drinking?

5
I don't reget my wine
I mourn the loss
Of my husband
Sir, you resemble him

6
Tell me, beautiful hostess
You had three children
By him
Now you have six

7
News came
That he was dead and burie
So I remarried

8
The brave sailor emptied
His glass, without thanks
Weeping, he returned
To his ship

Brave marin

ve marin revient de guerre
it doux (bis)
it mal chaussé, tout mal vêtu
ivre marin, d'où reviens-tu?
it doux

dame, je reviens de guerre,
it doux (bis)
on apporte ici du vin blanc
₂ le marin boive en passant
it doux

ve marin se met à boire
it doux (bis)
net à boire et à chanter
a belle hôtesse à pleurer
it doux

avez-vous donc,
 belle hôtesse
it doux (bis)
rettez-vous votre vin blanc
₂ le marin boit en passant?
it doux

5
C'est point mon vin
Que je regrette, tout doux (bis)
C'est la perte de mon mari
Monsieur, vous ressemblez à lui
Tout doux

6
Dites-moi donc, ah! belle hotesse
Tout doux (bis)
Vous aviez de lui trois enfants
Vous en avez six à présent ...
Tout doux

7
On m'a tant dit de ses nouvelles
Tout doux (bis)
Qu'il était mort et enterré...
Que je me suis remariée
Tout doux

8
Brave marin vida son verre
Tout doux (bis)
Sans remercier, tout en pleurant
A regagné son batiment
Tout doux

Monday morning

A repetitive march about every day of the week.

Monday morning
The emperor, his wife and the little prince
Came to my home
To shake hands with me
As I was out
The little prince said
Since that's the way it is
We'll come back on Tuesday

(Continue in the same manner, substituting the other days of the week)

Lundi matin

Lundi matin
L'emp'reur, sa femme et le p'tit prince
Sont venus chez moi
Pour me serrer la pince
Comme j'étais parti
Le p'tit prince a dit
Puisque c'est ainsi
Nous reviendrons mardi

(Continuer avec tous les jours de la semaine: mercredi, jeudi, vendredi, samedi, dimanche)

The king and the marquise

A dramatic song describing the tragic end of Gabrielle d'Estrées, who lived at the court of King Henri IV. The origin of this historical tune may date back as far as the 16th century.

1
The king ordered the drums to beat
To call out the ladies
And the first one he saw
Stole his soul

2
Marquis, tell me
Do you know her?
Who is this lovely lady?
The marquis answered
Sire, it's my wife

3
Marquis, you are luckier than me
To have such a beautiful wife
If you are willing to give her to me
I will take care of her

4
Sire, if you weren't the king
I'd demand retribution
But since you are the king
I will obey

5
Marquis, don't be angry
You'll have your reward
In my armies, I'll make you
Grand marshal of France

6
Farewell my love
Farewell my heart
Farewell my hope!
Since the king
Must be obeyed
Let's separate

7
The queen ordered
A special bouquet of
Beautiful lilies, and the
Aroma of that bouquet
Brought on the death
Of the marquise

Le roi et la marquise

1
Le roi a fait battre tambour (bis)
Pour voir toutes ces dames
Et la première qu'il a vue
Lui a ravi son âme

2
Marquis, dis-moi
La connais-tu? (bis)
Qui est cette jolie dame?
Le marquis lui a répondu
Sire roi, c'est ma femme

3
Marquis, tu es plus heureux
Qu'moi (bis)
D'avoir femme si belle
Si tu voulais me l'accorder
Je me chargerais d'elle

4
Sire, si vous n'étiez pas le roi (bis)
J'en tirerais vengeance
Mais puisque vous êtes le roi
A votre obéissance

5
Marquis, ne te fâche
Donc pas (bis)
Tu auras ta récompense
Je te ferai dans mes armées
Beau maréchal de France

6
Adieu ma mie
Adieu mon cœur (bis)
Adieu mon espérance!
Puisqu'il faut servir le roi
Séparons nous d'ensemble

7
La reine a fait faire
Un bouquet (bis)
De belles fleurs de lyse
Et la senteur de ce bouquet
A fait mourir marquise

The farewell song (Auld Lang Syne)

Here is the French version of "Auld Lang Syne." The original tune was composed in Scotland around 1750. The song has become traditional in France, especially with the Boy Scouts.

1
Must we leave one another
Without any hope of return
Must we leave one another
Without any hope of seeing each other again?

(refrain)
It's only a good-by, my brothers
It's only a good-by
Yes, we'll see each other again, my brothers
It's only a good-by

2
With our hands entwined
At twilight time
With our hands entwined
Let's fashion a chain of love

3
United by this gentle chain
All of us on this very spot
United by this gentle chain
Let's not say farewell

4
For God our witness
Blesses us
For God our witness
Will know to reunite us

Le chant des adieux

1
Faut-il nous quitter sans espoir
Sans espoir de retour
Faut-il nous quitter sans espoir
De nous revoir un jour?

(refrain)
Ce n'est qu'un au revoir, mes frères
Ce n'est qu'un au revoir
Oui, nous nous reverrons, mes frères
Ce n'est qu'un au revoir

2
Formons de nos mains qui s'enlacent
Au déclin de ce jour
Formons de nos mains qui s'enlacent
Une chaîne d'amour

3
Unis par cette douce chaîne
Tous, en ce même lieu
Unis par cette douce chaîne
Ne faisons point d'adieu

4
Car Dieu qui nous voit tous ensemble
Et qui va nous bénir
Car Dieu qui nous voit tous ensemble
Saura nous réunir

NOTES

www.ingramcontent.com/pod-product-compliance
Lightning Source LLC
Chambersburg PA
CBHW061247040426
42444CB00010B/2282